Unapologetically Being Me

A 21 Day Inspirational for Sustaining a Positive Outlook of Oneself in Spite of Criticism.

Tyra E. Rowell

Table of Contents

Introduction

Apology for What?

"So, can you explain to us the reason for your level of commitment not being like last year?" said the Principal. By this point, I was appalled by the Principal and the Executive Director accusing me of things that weren't true. When I was asked this question, all I could respond with was, "After all I have done for this school since August." I was already feeling ambushed and ready to walk out of the meeting. A meeting which I thought was to discuss preparations for the second semester. I knew something wasn't right, especially, when I kept repeating the scripture in my mind from the book of James, *"be swift to hear, slow to speak, and slow to anger."* Then, the big word came, *culminate.*

I have to be honest, I'm not eloquent in words and surely don't speak them articulately. I'm sitting there wondering to myself what in the world is *culminate.* As soon as I thought it, I responded, "What do you mean by culminate on the 18th?" The principal responded with the same sentence, "Your position will culminate on the 18th." I may be paraphrasing a little, but the most active word in my memory from that day is *culminate.* I responded quickly, "Are you firing me?" The principal responded, "Yes." I responded again, "So, you're firing me because my level of commitment is not like last year." The principal and the Executive Director shook their heads yes. I responded, "I understand and see clearly now. Thank you." I quickly got up and left the room. Be mindful, this was on a Wednesday when I was fired, the 18th wasn't until Friday. I had to go back to work for the next two days as if nothing had happened. I had to see my students who I have cared about deeply since day one and say nothing. I had to continue my duties as if nothing was changing. I had to speak and interact with the teachers as if Friday was not my last day. I was distraught and very hurt, especially by the fact that I was being fired for something that was not true. When I left that meeting, I hid in my office and cried for two hours questioning myself. *What could I have done so wrong to get fired? Did I say something wrong to a parent, teacher, or student? Was I late for work? Is it because of the way I talk? Could I have done more? Could I have kissed their behinds more? Could I have pretended a little more? Could I have not been so outspoken against things that weren't right? What for? That's not who I am. I am made the way I am. I can't believe they did this to me? Who do those people think they are? Why am I always being treated like I'm nothing? Do they not know who they just fired? Should I go back in there and apologize and beg for my job back?*

After two hours, I finally came to the conclusion that I did nothing wrong to deserve a termination from my job. Then, later that night I thought maybe it was for the best. No one knew that I had been praying daily since October of that school year for God to rescue me from that school. I was miserable. I was having heart palpitations from stress. I was gaining weight which was due to eating my favorite comfort foods. I was very irritated at home with my family and taking out my frustrations on them. In the midst of my physical complications, God did rescue me. It was in a way I never expected. The truth was I was never leaving because of the students. If I had never got fired, I would probably still be there miserably. I say all this, because this experience caused me to doubt myself in God. It caused me to look at myself in a negative way. I felt defeated that my reputation was ruined by my first termination as a School Counselor. I applied for other jobs and was rejected. I believed I wasn't good enough. One day this very thought came to my mind after an interview I thought was promising:

"Maybe I am. Maybe I'm not. But who are they to say what I'm not."

This thought led me back to 1 Corinthians 15:10 (ESV), *"But by the grace of God I am what I am, and His grace toward me was not in vain. On the contrary, I worked harder than any of them, though it was not I, but the grace of God that is with me."* I am so glad to know who I am.

The purpose of this book is to encourage you to be the person God created you to be. There is no need for you to pretend to be something you are not. If you don't like being around a crowd of people, don't be. It's okay to have one, two, or three friends you feel comfortable being around. If you don't like putting on a façade around people just to please them, you don't have to. It is okay to show people the real you. If you don't like doing things a certain way, you don't have to. It may just be the way God intended for you. Don't apologize or regret being you. No matter what you do, there will always be criticism from people who don't know anything about you. No one on this earth, including family and friends close to you, church family, colleagues, etc. have a right to make you feel inadequate or inferior. You were never created to be or feel inadequate or inferior. You were never created to be unhappy in this world. You were created to be victorious, great, and happy being the person God created you to be in the midst of a cynical society.

Who are you to believe you are not good enough for anything? God is not a God who regrets what He designs. He is a God who *fearfully and wonderfully* designed you just the way you are with all the flaws, imperfections, and limitations. Inadequacy is not a trait you were born with. Inadequacy is something you learn being brought into a world of criticism. And guess what? You can unlearn it. It doesn't matter if they said you wouldn't amount to anything. You can unlearn it. It doesn't matter if you've been rejected and/or abandoned. You can unlearn it. It doesn't matter if you were told you don't have the gift or anointing to do what God has called you to do. You can unlearn it. It doesn't matter if your evaluation at work entails you don't have what it takes. You can unlearn it. Any bad seed that was planted in your life can be unlearned! You have the power to turn that bad seed into a good seed through our Lord and Savior, Jesus Christ.

It is written in the Bible, *"I can do all things through Christ who strengthens me."* Philippians 4:13 (KJV). It is *your* privilege, *your* authority, and most definitely *your* responsibility to *speak* what is written, *do* what is written, and *live* what is written to enjoy *your* life to the fullest. Forget about what has been said about you. Forget about all the wrongs you have done in the past. Forget about all the wrongs that have even been done to you. You are no longer condemned by anything or what has been put forth in the universe by others. *You are in Christ Jesus walking after the Spirit and not after the flesh.* (Romans 8:1 KJV) Don't get it twisted. It is essential that you be walking and living your life through the Spirit and not the flesh to no longer be condemned. There's nothing good about the flesh, but *greater is He that is in you* (1 John 4:4) that makes you good in the eyes of God! When God sees you, He doesn't see you; He sees Jesus.

It is my sole desire that this book teaches you how to sustain a positive outlook on self and live a life you have been called to live in the eyes of God! And prayerfully, you will choose the life God has chosen for you to follow according to His Word! I pray you follow peace that surpasses all understanding, an assertiveness that speaks out in lovingkindness, a boldness that shows you know whose you are, and an abundant life that is full of love and laughter. I pray you will be set free, healed, restored, and delivered through the power of God's Word written in this book. I also pray you stand strong on His Word, O' mighty warrior of Christ! You are who God says you are! Give no room for Satan to use any vessel to speak lies over your life!

Your Daily Exercises

How many of you believe you can be made perfect through practice? There's nothing more that God would love from His people than to see them made perfect in His eyes. In reality, perfection takes practice. Each day you are to complete the daily exercises to be made perfect through practice. These exercises will also help you embrace or adopt what God is saying about you so you can conquer inadequacy, inferiority, and/or insecurity in spite of criticism. Please take the time to put in the work, because faith without work is dead. You will be blessed with the outcome! Examples of the exercises are as followed:

Exchange of Thoughts:
"How precious also are thy thoughts unto me, O' God! How great is the sum of them! Psalms 139: 17 (KJV)

God's thoughts are not our thoughts. The negative thoughts that you may have of yourself are not the thoughts that God has about you. Precious thoughts are not the ones that hurt, belittle, and/or demeanor you. Precious thoughts build you up, make you feel loved, and set you free. *This exercise is for you to swap out your negative thoughts for what God thinks of you.*

For example:
My thought: I am afraid. I can't do this.
God's thought: Do not be afraid. I didn't give you the spirit of fear, but of love, power, and a sound mind.

A Proclamation to Self: *This exercise is for you to proclaim or make a bold statement to remind yourself of the things God want you to know about yourself.*

For example:
Tyra, you are victorious on this day for taking a step further in your writing in spite of your fear of failure and the unknown. Write, Wait, and Watch God move! He gets all the glory!

Write It Down and See It: *This exercise is for you to hide the Word in your heart through memorization. First, find the scripture and fill in the blanks. Second, write one word, phrase, or sentence from the verse that prophesy or stand out to you. Third, write that one word, phrase, or sentence on your mirror in the bathroom, in your journal, on a sticky note, or in your cell phone to remember or refer back to it.*

For example:
One verse: Isaiah 64: 8 (ESV)

"But now, O Lord, you are our <u>Father</u>; we are the <u>clay</u>, and you are our <u>potter</u>; we are all the <u>work of your hand</u>."

One word, phrase, or sentence:
<u>God made me.</u>

It's time to Talk: *This exercise is for you to enjoy talking to God about anything that is on your mind and in your heart. Keep these five key points in mind when talking to God:*
1.   *Acknowledge Him and tell Him who He is to you.*
2.   *Ask Him to forgive you for any shortcomings in your life.*
3.   *Give Him thanks for everything, including the things that may be difficult or a struggle in your life.*
4.   *Tell Him what you need, ask Him freely, and believe that He will give it to you. Because after all, you are His child.*
5.   *Seal it, stamp it, and declare it in His Son, Jesus's name!*

For example:
My Heavenly Father, you are so Awesome to me. I am glad to call you Daddy for You have always been there for me. Even when I felt like I was so alone, You were with me. I pray Lord that You forgive me for all my shortcomings for I desire to not sin against You. I thank You Lord for being my Provider and making a way for me even when I don't see the way. I may not have a job right now, but I am surely glad to be working for You writing this book. I don't know how my bills will be paid, but I trust You Lord. I don't know how the book will turn out, but I trust You Lord. I pray Lord for strength to complete the task You have given me. I pray Lord that I write what You want me to write. I pray Lord that each individual who buys this book will be transformed by Your Word. I pray this prayer in my Lord and Savior, Jesus Christ's name! Amen!

I am

I am who God says I am.
I am made the way God designed me.
I love being me.
I don't like faking in front of people.
I like speaking to people even when they don't speak back.
I like smiling even when others don't smile back.
I love being me even though I can't hear a fire alarm.
I love being me even though I don't' speak eloquently.
I love being the person God created me to be.
I am anointed.
I am qualified.
I am His Child.
I am royalty and don't care who don't believe it.
I am that I am
through the grace of God and can't nobody change that.
I refuse to apologize for being me.
If anyone have a problem with me being the way I am,
I suggest they take it up with God.

In His Likeness

Day 1

Be Aware of Whose You Are

"Because you are His sons, God sent the Spirit of His Son into our hearts, the Spirit who calls out, "Abba, Father." So you are no longer a slave, but God's Child; and since you are His child, God has made you also an heir."
Galatians 4:6-7 (NIV)

SONS AND DAUGHTERS OF GOD, be well-versed in whose you are. You are God's child. Yes, you were conceived by your earthly mother and father, but you are still God's child. Since you are His, you are also an heir entitled to an inheritance. An inheritance of abundant peace and eternal life. Through faith, you can live happy, whole, and free. If you are not happy, know that God can give you an unspeakable joy that the world can't give to you. If you are not whole, know that God is able to mend you back together, no matter the circumstances. Isaiah 64:8 says, *"Yet you, LORD, are our Father. We are the clay, you are the potter; we are all the work of your hand."* If you are feeling trapped and in bondage, give your life to Jesus for He is the One who can set you free. *For whom the Lord sets free is free indeed.* (John 8:36) Choose this day to be free! Believe, confess with your mouth and surrender your all to Jesus Christ!

"Little children, you are from God and have overcome them, for He who is in you is Greater than he that is in the world." 1 John 4: 4 (ESV)

Child of God, stand boldly and let others know who your Daddy is! For Greater is He that is in you. Do you not know how great your Daddy is?! Do you not know how much greatness He has placed in you?! Greatness that is beyond what you could ever think of yourself. *You are awesome! You are bold. You are courageous. You are daring. You are enough. You are forgiven. You are great. You are happy. You are igniting. You are just. You are kind. You are loved. You are merciful. You are nonstop. You are outstanding. You are protected. You are qualified. You are respectful. You are strong. You are totally beautiful or handsome. You are useful. You are valuable. You are a warrior. You are X-excellence. You are youthful. You are a zealous fan of Christ.*

"The earth is the Lord's, and the fullness thereof; the world, and they that dwell therein." Psalms 24:1 (KJV)

This scripture says it all. You belong to God and the safest place to be is in His Hands. I encourage you to give Him a chance to be your all and all. Whatever you need Him to be in your life, He can be. If you need a father, He can be that for you. If you need a mother, He can be that for you. If you need a Provider, He can be that for you. If you need a Protector, He can be that for you. If you need Him to make Provisions for you, He can do that, too. Once again, He can be whatever you need Him to be in your life! You have to communicate that to Him. Yes, He is an omniscient (knows all and sees all) God, but He still wants to hear it from you who has a free will.

Your Daily Exercises

Exchange of Thoughts: *This exercise is for you to swap out your negative thoughts for what God thinks of you.*

What thought(s) are you having in regards to who and whose you are?

Your thought:

God's thought:

A Proclamation to Self: *This exercise is for you to proclaim or make a bold statement to remind yourself of whose you are.*

(Your name), you are....

_____.

Write It Down and See It: *This exercise is for you to hide the Word in your heart through memorization.*
- *(1) First, find the scripture below and fill in the blanks.*
- *(2) Second, write one word, phrase, or sentence from the verse that prophesy or stand out to you.*
- *(3) Third, write that one word, phrase, or sentence on your mirror in the bathroom, in your journal, on a sticky note, or in your cell phone to remember or refer back to it.*

1 John 3:1 (ESV)
One verse: *"See what kind of _____ the Father has given to us that we should be called _____ of God; and so we are! The reason why the world does not _____ us is that it did not _____ Him.*

One word, phrase, or sentence:
_____

It's time to Talk: *This exercise is for you to enjoy talking to God anywhere and anytime about anything that is on your mind. You are welcome to write your prayer on the lines provided below. Keep these five key points in mind when talking to God:*
1. *Acknowledge Him and tell Him who He is to you.*
2. *Ask Him to forgive you for any shortcomings in your life.*

3. *Give Him thanks for everything including the things that may be difficult or a struggle in your life.*
4. *Tell Him what you need, ask Him freely, and believe that He will give it to you. Because after all, you are His child.*
5. *Seal it, stamp it, and declare it in His Son, Jesus's name!*

_____

_____

_____

_____

_____

_____

_____

_____

_____

Day 2

You were Never Created to be Inadequate

"So God created man in His own image, in the image of God He created him; male and female He created them." Genesis 1:27 (ESV)

CHILD OF GOD, you are not inadequate, because your Daddy in Heaven is not inadequate. You are a reflection of Him. You were made in His image. When you look in the mirror, you are to smile and admire the One who made you. It isn't beneficial to you to acknowledge all the imperfections and flaws. The mirror should be a tool for you to admire the One who made you. He made you in the likeness of Him. Let's be clear, though. That doesn't mean you have total superior powers like God, but you do have victory already over every situation. You have victory, because you serve a victorious God who you have (prayerfully) given total control over your life. He knew you before your mom and dad even thought to get together. He knows your weaknesses as well as your strengths. There is not a thought you could hide from Him. There's not a wrinkle you could cover up as if He doesn't already know. There's not a bald spot he doesn't already see. He knows you from your head to your toe. He also knows your past, present, and future. He knows the decisions you will make in the future. He already knows. So, since He already knows, there's no point in acknowledging your imperfections and flaws. They do not make you less of a man, woman, boy, or girl in His eyesight. Not one bit less!

"But God chose what is foolish in the world to shame the wise; God chose what is weak in the world to shame the strong." 1 Corinthians 1:27 (ESV)

In Exodus the third and fourth chapter (NIV), God chose Moses to lead His people from the oppression of Pharaoh in Egypt. Moses's first reply was, "Who am I to go to Pharaoh and bring the children of Israel out of Egypt?" God replied, "I will be with you and this shall be the sign for you that I have sent you." Moses replied the second time, "If I go to the people telling them the God of their fathers has sent me, and they ask what his name is, what shall I say to them?" God replied to Moses, "I Am who I Am. Say to the children of Israel, I Am has sent me to you." God continued to give Moses more instructions on what to tell His people. He also let Moses know that He already knew that Pharaoh was not going to let the children of Israel go until He struck Egypt with wonders and plagues. Moses replied the third time, "They will not believe me?" God gave him instructions on different signs of wonders to use so they will believe him. Moses replied the fourth time, "I am not eloquent. I am slow of speech and slow of tongue." God replied, "Who made man's mouth? Who makes him mute, or deaf, or seeing, or blind? Is it not I, the Lord? Now, go, I will be with your mouth and teach you what you shall speak." Moses replied the fifth time, "Lord, is there someone else you can send?" God got a little angry with Moses, but He gave instructions to him that Aaron will be with him and He will use both of their mouths to speak what needs to be said.

Have you ever asked this question of yourself when God gave you a task to complete. *Who am I?*

Who are you? You are the one God chose to complete that task He has asked you to do. Whatever He asked of you to do, He has already put in you the things you need to complete it. It's impossible to be inadequate in something God has equipped and ordained you to perform. You can run from it and decide not to do it. You can even try to talk God out of it like Moses, but you will perform that task God has chosen you to do. The next time you are summoned to complete a task, don't second-guess yourself. Don't feel like you are not adequate enough to do the job. Don't try to talk yourself out of it. God know you and has already equipped you with the gifts, strategies, and resources to complete the task. Don't miss another opportunity to glorify God with what He has already placed inside of you. You are good enough! Yes, you!

Your Daily Exercises

Exchange of Thoughts: *This exercise is for you to swap out your negative thoughts for what God thinks of you.*

What thought(s) are you having when God ask you to do something that is not comfortable to you?

Your thought:

God's thought:

A Proclamation to Self: *This exercise is for you to proclaim or make a bold statement to remind yourself that you are good enough to complete your God-given task.*

(Your name), you are....

_____.

Write It Down and See It: *This exercise is for you to hide the Word in your heart through memorization.*
>   (1) *First, find the scripture below and fill in the blanks.*
>   (2) *Second, write one word, phrase, or sentence from the verse that prophesy or stand out to you.*
>   (3) *Third, write that one word, phrase, or sentence on your mirror in the bathroom, in your journal, on a sticky note, or in your cell phone to remember or refer back to it.*

Ephesians 2:10 (NIV)

One verse: *"For we are God's_____, created in Christ Jesus to do good works, which God prepared in _____ for us to do."*

One word, phrase, or sentence:

_____

It's time to Talk: *This exercise is for you to enjoy talking to God anywhere and anytime about anything that is on your mind. You are welcome to write your prayer on the lines provided below. Keep these five key points in mind when talking to God:*

1. *Acknowledge Him and tell Him who He is to you.*
2. *Ask Him to forgive you for any shortcomings in your life.*
3. *Give Him thanks for everything including the things that may be difficult or a struggle in your life.*
4. *Tell Him what you need, ask Him freely, and believe that He will give it to you. Because after all, you are His child.*
5. *Seal it, stamp it, and declare it in His Son, Jesus's name!*

_____
_____
_____
_____
_____
_____
_____
_____
_____
_____

Day 3

It is God who Justified You

"And those He predestined, He also called; those He called, He also justified; those He justified, He also glorified. What, then, shall we say in response to these things? If God is for us, who can be against us?"
Romans 8:30-31 (NIV)

OFTENTIMES, YOU WILL hear people criticize you for doing things a certain way. They would complain and wonder why you have been called to do what you do. They would look at you as if you were doing something so outrageous. Some people would even have the audacity to get mad at you just because you are doing what God has called you to do. To be honest, it's not them, it's only the enemy mad about it. If someone wants to be used as a naysayer, let them. Just remember, *you are **not** fighting against flesh and blood.* (Ephesians 6:12)

Paul said, "If God is for us, who can be against us?" This means no one can stop what God has put forth to be accomplished. All you need to know is that when God picks you to complete a task for His glory, know that He justified you. In my opinion, *justify* means, to approve someone worthy or righteous. Man does not justify, because too much energy is being spent on appearances (how a person looks). Don't pay any mind to others' criticism. Remember, it's only the devil who is mad about it. Whatever God gives you to complete, do it in excellence without fear. *For our God did not give us the spirit of fear, but of Love, Power, and a Sound Mind.* (2 Timothy 1:7)

In 1 Samuel the sixteenth chapter (NIV), Samuel was summoned to go see Jesse the Bethlehemite to appoint a king over the children of Israel. Samuel replied, "How can I go? If Saul finds out, he will kill me."

Just to pause for a moment here. When God asks us to do something, it's okay to ask questions. He will answer. I don't think, in my opinion, Samuel was trying to get out of it like Moses, but I do think he was afraid Saul would kill him. I just want to take this moment to bring out a point that no matter what may be going on in your life, you can ask God about it. He will give you the course of action to take to complete the assignment in spite of the circumstance.

Back to the reason for Samuel being sent to Jesse. Samuel went and did what God told him to do. Samuel went to Jesse and had all the sons line up for the sacrifice. David was in the field tending to the sheep. Samuel first looked at Eliab and thought to himself, *Surely the Lord is anointing him*. God said to Samuel, "Do not look at his appearance or on the height of his stature, because I have rejected him. For the Lord sees not as man sees; man looks on the outward appearance, but the Lord looks on the heart." Eventually, all the sons came before Samuel and every single one was rejected. Samuel asked Jesse if all his sons were there. Jesse stated the youngest was not there for he was in the field tending to sheep. Samuel sent for him and waited for the youngest to come. David, the youngest son, was brought in and God told Samuel to anoint him for he was the king.

The reason for sharing this story from the bible is to show you that it is God who justifies and qualifies who He wishes to complete a task for His glory. David was chosen after God's own heart. Surely, people wondered (even I wondered) why God picked David when He knew He would be a murderer and a cheater. It's not our job to question who God approves. He is the only One who knows our hearts. He doesn't look at our appearance when choosing us either, but man does.

Your Daily Exercises

Exchange of Thoughts: *This exercise is for you to swap out your negative thoughts for what God thinks of you.*

What thought(s) are you having when you are faced with obstacles of criticism (from either yourself or others) when you are picked to complete a God-given task?

Your thought:

God's thought:

A Proclamation to Self: *This exercise is for you to proclaim or make a bold statement to remind yourself that God is one who called or justified you to complete a task.*

(Your name), you are....

_____.

Write It Down and See It: *This exercise is for you to hide the Word in your heart through memorization.*
    (1) *First, find the scripture below and fill in the blanks.*
    (2) *Second, write one word, phrase, or sentence from the verse that prophesy or stand out to you.*
    (3) *Third, write that one word, phrase, or sentence on your mirror in the bathroom, in your journal, on a sticky note, or in your cell phone to remember or refer back to it.*

Ephesians 2:10 (NIV)
One verse: *"For we are God's_____, created in Christ Jesus to do good works, which God prepared in _____ for us to do."*

One word, phrase, or sentence:

_____

It's time to Talk: *This exercise is for you to enjoy talking to God anywhere and anytime about anything that is on your mind. You are welcome to write your prayer on the lines provided below. Keep these five key points in mind when talking to God:*

1. *Acknowledge Him and tell Him who He is to you.*
2. *Ask Him to forgive you for any shortcomings in your life.*
3. *Give Him thanks for everything including the things that may be difficult or a struggle in your life.*
4. *Tell Him what you need, ask Him freely, and believe that He will give it to you. Because after all, you are His child.*
5. *Seal it, stamp it, and declare it in His Son, Jesus's name!*

_____

_____

_____

_____

_____

_____

_____

_____

_____

_____

Day 4

You Have Access to God

"For through Him we both have access by one Spirit unto the Father."
Ephesians 2:18 (KJV)

THANKS BE TO Jesus Christ, that you have access to God! You don't have to rely on the pastor of the church to tell you what God is saying to you. You don't have to rely on a friend or co-worker to go to God for you. You don't have to ask the neighbor to send a prayer for you. *The veil has been shredded to pieces because Jesus died on the cross.* (Matthew 27:51). In the Old Testament, the people of God had to go through a priest for redemption of their sins or to hear from God. Today, there is nothing stopping you from talking to God, but you. Have no fear or doubts! *You can go boldly to the throne of grace and make known your request through Jesus Christ!* (Hebrews 10:19-22)

With that being said, you have access to talk to God anywhere at any given time. You could be in the midst of a storm or circumstance in your life, and send up a prayer without opening your mouth. God is just that good! He can hear your thoughts! You have no reason to not know what God desires of you because *His Word says if you draw near to Him, He will draw near to you.* (James 4:8) Which literally means, He will have a conversation with you either through dreams, mind, visions, circumstances, or sometimes through others. God has an open door policy!

Just to share a testimony. As a child, I was brought up in church and learned who God was and is to me. We had conversations a lot when I was a child, because I hated the way I was made. I can even remember my first book in the Bible I read which was John the first chapter, verses one through three (KJV). *"In the beginning was the Word, and the Word was with God, and the Word was God. The same was in the beginning with God. All things were made by Him, and without Him was not anything made that was made."* As a teenager in high school, I learned to appreciate the way I was made in God's image. I also learned that nothing or no one could stop me from doing what God would have me to do.

In my early twenties, I was introduced to Jesus Christ and I surrendered my life to Him. During this period of my life, I was introduced as a babe in Christ and told many lies by my Pastors that they claimed God had told them to tell me. I was a babe in Christ, but I knew the voice of God. I also knew His Word, too. You couldn't make me doubt Him after He had brought me through molestation, ridicule, suicidal thoughts, negativity, and verbal abuse as a child. Yet, somehow, I listened and believed every word that proceeded out of their mouths. Eventually, I felt trapped and in bondage because I found myself going to these Pastors when I had a problem instead of going directly to God. I prayed and prayed for God to give me a way of an escape. One thing I learned about myself is that I love being free. Free to do whatever I choose to do. My passion for freedom is what brought me out of my situation. When I left, I wasn't like Lot's wife looking back. I ran like Tina Turner did (in the movie) when she left Ike. I ran and didn't look back. I felt free. Singing what Dr. Martin Luther King, Jr. said, *"Free at last. Free at last. Thank God Almighty I am free at last."*

"Now the Lord is the Spirit: and where the Spirit of the Lord is, there is freedom." 2 Corinthians 3:17 (ESV)

I share all this to say that God is accessible to you. You can cry, kneel, or lie on the floor in the comfort of your home, office, or church. God will hear you. Today, tell God what you need. God is just that good! If you don't know Jesus, I pray you will confess and make Him your Lord and Savior today. *He is the way, the truth, and the life. No one comes to the Father except through Him.* (John 14:6). He is waiting for you. He desires no one to be bound!

Your Daily Exercises

Exchange of Thoughts: *This exercise is for you to swap out your negative thoughts for what God thinks of you.*

What thought(s) are you having when you are driven to talk to someone else about your problems instead of talking to God?

Your thought:

God's thought:

A Proclamation to Self: *This exercise is for you to proclaim or make a bold statement to remind yourself that you can boldly go to God in confidence about your situation.*

(Your name), you are....

_____.

Write It Down and See It: *This exercise is for you to hide the Word in your heart through memorization.*
- (1) *First, find the scripture below and fill in the blanks.*
- (2) *Second, write one word, phrase, or sentence from the verse that prophesy or stand out to you.*
- (3) *Third, write that one word, phrase, or sentence on your mirror in the bathroom, in your journal, on a sticky note, or in your cell phone to remember or refer back to it.*

Psalms 120:1 (KJV)

One verse: *"In my distress, I _____ to the Lord, and He _____ me."*

One word, phrase, or sentence:

_____

It's time to Talk: *This exercise is for you to enjoy talking to God anywhere and anytime about anything that is on your mind. You are welcome to write your prayer on the lines provided below. Keep these five key points in mind when talking to God:*

1. *Acknowledge Him and tell Him who He is to you.*
2. *Ask Him to forgive you for any shortcomings in your life.*
3. *Give Him thanks for everything including the things that may be difficult or a struggle in your life.*
4. *Tell Him what you need, ask Him freely, and believe that He will give it to you. Because after all, you are His child.*
5. *Seal it, stamp it, and declare it in His Son, Jesus's name!*

_____

_____

_____

_____

_____

_____

_____

_____

_____

_____

Day 5

God is with You

"Fear not, for I am with you; be not dismayed, for I am your God; I will strengthen you, I will help you, I will uphold you with my righteous right hand." Isaiah 41:10 (ESV)

IT DOESN'T MATTER where you live or where you go on a daily basis, God is with you. *He will never leave you or forsake you.* (Deuteronomy 31:6 NIV) You will have to be the one to leave God, because it is not His character to leave you. He loves you too much to leave you alone. Whether you are at an interview, driving on the highway, washing dishes, or just watching television, know that God is with you. Be confident in your faith of knowing God is with you. He has your back and when you are in tune with Him, He will make sure you are not being ambushed. His people know His voice and those who love Him obey His voice. God doesn't want you to live your life in fear of what others think of you or what others will do to you. God is with you every step of the way and He wants to be there for you. So let Him!

Remember the story of Moses when God summoned him to go to Egypt. What did God tell him numerous times? That He will be there with him. Have you ever had an experience in your life where you were about to go to an unknown place? You either asked a family or church member to go with you. Do you remember how you felt when that person showed up and stayed with you until the end? Then, you will feel ten times better knowing God is with you. Especially someone whom you cannot see, but yet believe! (I got my shouting shoes on.) God is just that good!

In Judges the sixth chapter, the children of Israel were held captive in the hands of the Midianites for doing such evil in the eyes of the Lord. One day an angel of the Lord appeared to Gideon who was beating out wheat in a winepress. He was in the winepress hiding the wheat from the Midianites because they devoured everything that the children of Israel grew on the land. The children of Israel had been crying out to God to save them. The angel of God told Gideon that he will save the children of Israel from the Midianites. Gideon replied, "How can I save Israel? My clan is the weakest in Manasseh, and I am the least in my father's house." The angel of God responded, "I will be with you and you will strike the Midianites as one man." As the story continues on, Gideon's army went from 10,000 to 300 men to fight a large army of Midianites. Gideon stepped out on faith in God defeating the Midianites.

What message(s) did you get from the sixth chapter in Judges?

_____

_____

_____

_____

_____

The messages I got from this chapter in Judges:

(1) When you disobey God, you will suffer the consequences.

(2) I am not the only one who had negative self-images. Gideon thought negative of himself, too. But God didn't see him that way. He called Gideon a warrior.

(3) God is with you and when He is with you, you are GUARANTEED to win!

Your Daily Exercises

Exchange of Thoughts: *This exercise is for you to swap out your negative thoughts for what God thinks of you.*
What thought(s) are you having when you are in an unfamiliar or unknown place to complete a God-given task.

Your thought:

God's thought:

A Proclamation to Self: *This exercise is for you to proclaim or make a bold statement to remind yourself that God is with you.*

(Your name), you are....

_____.

Write It Down and See It: *This exercise is for you to hide the Word in your heart through memorization.*
   (1) *First, find the scripture below and fill in the blanks.*
   (2) *Second, write one word, phrase, or sentence from the verse that prophesy or stand out to you.*
   (3) *Third, write that one word, phrase, or sentence on your mirror in the bathroom, in your journal, on a sticky note, or in your cell phone to remember or refer back to it.*

Isaiah 59:1 (NIV)
One verse: *"Behold, the Lord's Hand is not shortened, that it cannot _____, or his ear dull, that it cannot _____."*

One word, phrase, or sentence:
_____

It's time to Talk: *This exercise is for you to enjoy talking to God anywhere and anytime about anything that is on your mind. You are welcome to write your prayer on the lines provided below. Keep these five key points in mind when talking to God:*

1. *Acknowledge Him and tell Him who He is to you.*
2. *Ask Him to forgive you for any shortcomings in your life.*
3. *Give Him thanks for everything including the things that may be difficult or a struggle in your life.*
4. *Tell Him what you need, ask Him freely, and believe that He will give it to you. Because after all, you are His child.*
5. *Seal it, stamp it, and declare it in His Son, Jesus's name!*

_____

_____

_____

_____

_____

_____

_____

_____

_____

_____

Day 6
Surrender to His Love for You

"No, in all these things we are more than conquerors through Him who loved us. For I am sure that neither death nor life, nor angels nor rulers, nor things present nor things to come, nor powers, nor height nor depth, nor anything else in all creation, will be able to separate us from the love of God in Christ Jesus our Lord." Romans 8:37-39 (ESV)

THERE IS NOTHING you could ever do or not do that will make God stop loving you. If someone told you otherwise, he or she is lying to you. God will love you all the way to hell if that's where you choose to go. Nothing should come between the love of God and His children. Just like there's' nothing that could come between the love of a mother and her child.

God cares about you. If He didn't, He wouldn't have sent His only Son to die for your sins so that you may live life abundantly. If you ever want to know what it feels like to be loved, surrender to the love of Christ. He was hanged on the cross and endured the persecution and torture to His body for you and me. There is no other love like the love of Christ who died for His friends. God loves you! I cannot emphasize that enough, but be assured God loves you even in spite of your circumstances or difficulties in life. Your circumstances should not be the downfall of your life. Your past hurt should not be the focus of your life. Someone told me that there is always someone else who has had it worse than me. I have seen people be healed from the worst of situations and they don't look anywhere near what they have been through. That's why some people call them survivors. However, I call them *conquerors*!

"Because of the Lord's great love, we are not consumed, for compassions never fail." Lamentations 3:22 (NIV)

"Give thanks to the Lord; for He is good. For His steadfast love endures forever." Psalms 136:1-2 (ESV)

Lift up your heads, children of God!
Be lifted up!
Walk with your head up not down.
Walk with love in your hearts.
Walk with a praise on your lip continuously.
Walk with an assurance that you know without a doubt you are loved!

As I said before there is NOTHING you could ever do or not do that will make God stop loving you. God will love you all the way to hell if that's where you choose to go. Remember, God is love and love is God. When you have love reigning in life, you will love all God's people. Hate is not a characteristic of God. So, love your neighbor and your enemies too. If you find fault with them, go to them and make peace. If they don't want to hear what you have to say, leave in peace, because you did what God required of you.

Your Daily Exercises

Exchange of Thoughts: *This exercise is for you to swap out your negative thoughts for what God thinks of you.*

What thought(s) are you having when you know someone doesn't want to be in your company?

Your thought:

God's thought:

A Proclamation to Self: *This exercise is for you to proclaim or make a bold statement to remind yourself that you are loved.*

(Your name), you are....

_____.

Write It Down and See It: *This exercise is for you to hide the Word in your heart through memorization.*
    (1) *First, find the scripture below and fill in the blanks.*
    (2) *Second, write one word, phrase, or sentence from the verse that prophesy or stand out to you.*
    (3) *Third, write that one word, phrase, or sentence on your mirror in the bathroom, in your journal, on a sticky note, or in your cell phone to remember or refer back to it.*

1 Peter 5:7 (KJV)
One verse: *"Casting all your care upon Him; for He _____ for you."*

One word, phrase, or sentence:

_____

It's time to Talk: *This exercise is for you to enjoy talking to God anywhere and anytime about anything that is on your mind. You are welcome to write your prayer on the lines provided below. Keep these five key points in mind when talking to God:*
    1. *Acknowledge Him and tell Him who He is to you.*
    2. *Ask Him to forgive you for any shortcomings in your life.*

3. *Give Him thanks for everything including the things that may be difficult or a struggle in your life.*

4. *Tell Him what you need, ask Him freely, and believe that He will give it to you. Because after all, you are His child.*

5. *Seal it, stamp it, and declare it in His Son, Jesus's name!*

_____

_____

_____

_____

_____

_____

_____

_____

_____

_____

Day 7

You were made for Him

"For by Him were all things created, that are in heaven, and that are in earth, visible and invisible, whether they be thrones, or dominions, or principalities, or powers; all things were created by Him, and for Him."
Colossians 1:16 (KJV)

ALL THINGS WERE created by God and for God. God, the *Great I am*, created everything for Himself. For His purpose. For His glory. In His likeness. In His image. He has a purpose for everything moving and not moving in the heavens and on earth. With that being said, you were also created for Him and His purpose. Whether you fulfill that purpose or not, you are still His *workmanship*. (Ephesians 2:10) You are the *clay* and He's the *Potter*. He will always get the glory from whichever way you choose to live your life. Another note to take from this scripture is love your body that God has created. Love every flaw you think you have or not have. Love every dimple. Love every cellulite or firmness on your body. Love the straightness, crookedness, or gap in your teeth. Love the thinness or thickness of your hair. Love every limp or swish in your walk. Love every shape and form of your body. Love it if no one else does. Don't allow anyone else to point out imperfections about your body. If they have an issue with the way you look, tell them to take it up with the Lord!

Your Daily Exercises

Exchange of Thoughts: *This exercise is for you to swap out your negative thoughts for what God thinks of you.*

What thought(s) are you having when you see your full body (nakedness) in the mirror?

Your thought:

God's thought:

A Proclamation to Self: *This exercise is for you to proclaim or make a bold statement to remind yourself that you were made for God.*

(Your name), you are....

_____.

Write It Down and See It: *This exercise is for you to hide the Word in your heart through memorization.*
  (1) *First, find the scripture below and fill in the blanks.*
  (2) *Second, write one word, phrase, or sentence from the verse that prophesy or stand out to you.*
  (3) *Third, write that one word, phrase, or sentence on your mirror in the bathroom, in your journal, on a sticky note, or in your cell phone to remember or refer back to it.*

1 Corinthians 8:6 (NIV)
One verse: *"But to us there is but one _____, the Father, of whom are _____ things, and we in Him; and one Lord Jesus Christ, by whom are _____ things, and we by Him."*

One word, phrase, or sentence:

_____

It's time to Talk: *This exercise is for you to enjoy talking to God anywhere and anytime about anything that is on your mind. You are welcome to write your prayer on the lines provided below. Keep these five key points in mind when talking to God:*

1. *Acknowledge Him and tell Him who He is to you.*
2. *Ask Him to forgive you for any shortcomings in your life.*
3. *Give Him thanks for everything including the things that may be difficult or a struggle in your life.*
4. *Tell Him what you need, ask Him freely, and believe that He will give it to you. Because after all, you are His child.*
5. *Seal it, stamp it, and declare it in His Son, Jesus's name!*

_____
_____
_____
_____
_____
_____
_____
_____
_____
_____

Quench the Lies, not the Spirit

Day 8

Be Quick to Listen before Responding

"My dear brothers and sisters, take note of this: Everyone should be **QUICK TO LISTEN,** *slow to speak and slow to become angry."* James 1:19 (NIV)

BEING LIED ON or misunderstood is inevitable. It's going to happen. God is holding you responsible for knowing how to react when things are spoken about you that are not true. So, react by quenching the lies instead of quenching the Spirit. Quench, according to *dictionary.reference.com,* means to put out or extinguish. There are lies being spoken in the atmosphere against you and surely has no merit, but to make you doubt God. These type of lies need to be put out like fire or the flame of lies will spread. Lies can take hold of a person's mind by first entering the ears, but once it takes hold of the mind it can take root in the heart. Once it's rooted, it will be tended to like it's the absolute truth by being defensive, responding with contempt, and getting angry at times.

You don't have to believe every word that proceeds out of people's mouths. Especially people who are cynical and love to belittle others. At times, you may hear things about you from people who you may think are not cynical. The Word says, *try the spirit and see if it's of God* (1 John 4:1

KJV). You have to take the time to listen and test the spirit of those who are talking to you. While you are listening you will know if what they are saying or prophesying to you is or not of God. When you are quick to listen instead of responding, it gives you a chance to check in with God. God can hear your thoughts and when you are talking to him, He will give you instructions or strategies on how to respond or react. You quench the lies and not the Spirit by not saying what you really want to say, but saying what God tells you to say. What you really want to say may not be the right thing to say.

In my introduction of this book, I shared my experience of the day I got terminated from my job. I also shared the scripture that got me through the meeting which is the same scripture of this day. Well, let me share with you what I really wanted to say to the bosses. *Ok, so you're firing me for something you know nothing about. Talking about I have no commitment to this job. You of all people should know what that is like, because I don't see you doing anything but having meaningless meetings day in and day out with your administrative team. All talk but no walk. Too many Chiefs but no Indians.* I can go on and on and on. I have a few curse words to add, too. But as I look back over just the few lines of what I really wanted to say, they were not beneficial for me to say them. If I had said those things, what could have happened to me? What could have happened to the bosses? They would have probably gotten angry and called the police to escort me out that day. I don't know, but I'm glad I didn't say anything. I'm glad I didn't defend myself, either. I don't owe anyone an explanation about anything. I know I did my job to the best of my ability and gave all I had until it was time to exit the building. I have a clear conscience and no ill feelings toward anyone because I now know my termination was ordained by God. I am happy because He made a way of escape for me.

Your Daily Exercises

Exchange of Thoughts: *This exercise is for you to swap out your negative thoughts for what God thinks of you.*

What thought(s) are you having when someone is telling you something you know is not true about you?

Your thought:

God's thought:

A Proclamation to Self: *This exercise is for you to proclaim or make a bold statement to remind yourself to be quick to listen and not respond.*

(Your name), you are....

_____.

Write It Down and See It: *This exercise is for you to hide the Word in your heart through memorization.*
- (1) *First, find the scripture below and fill in the blanks.*
- (2) *Second, write one word, phrase, or sentence from the verse that prophesy or stand out to you.*
- (3) *Third, write that one word, phrase, or sentence on your mirror in the bathroom, in your journal, on a sticky note, or in your cell phone to remember or refer back to it.*

Job 12:11 (NIV)
One verse: *"Does not the _____ test words as the _____ tastes food?*

One word, phrase, or sentence:
_____

It's time to Talk: *This exercise is for you to enjoy talking to God anywhere and anytime about anything that is on your mind. You are* welcome to write your prayer on the lines provided below. Keep these five key points in mind when talking to God:

1. Acknowledge Him and tell Him who He is to you.
2. Ask Him to forgive you for any shortcomings in your life.
3. Give Him thanks for everything including the things that may be difficult or a struggle in your life.
4. Tell Him what you need, ask Him freely, and believe that He will give it to you. Because after all, you are His child.
5. Seal it, stamp it, and declare it in His Son, Jesus's name!

_____
_____
_____
_____
_____
_____
_____
_____
_____
_____
_____

Day 9
Let Silence be Your Friend

*"My dear brothers and sisters, take note of this: Everyone should be quick to listen, **SLOW TO SPEAK** and slow to become angry."* James 1:19 (NIV)

IT TAKES STRENGTH to be silent when all you want to do is open your mouth and say whatever pleases the flesh. With that being said, taking the road to be silent is not a weakness. Being silent is an advantage. Being silent keeps you. Being silent sustains you. Being silent makes sure you are not put to shame. Being silent gives you the opportunity to talk to God. Being silent also gives God the opportunity to tell you what to say.

There were times when Jesus remained silent when he was asked a question. For example, in Matthew the 27th chapter starting at verse eleven (ESV), Jesus was asked by the governor if He was the king of the Jews. Jesus replied, "You have said so." When the chief priests and elders started accusing him, he said not a word. Then, the governor, Pilate, asked Jesus, "Do you not hear how many things they testify against you?" Jesus didn't say a word. Pilate was "greatly amazed." In John the 8th chapter, a woman caught in adultery was brought to Jesus by the Pharisees. They said to him, "This woman was caught in adultery. In the Law of Moses we are commanded to stone this woman. What do you say?" Jesus didn't say a word. He just kneeled down and started writing on the ground with his finger. The Pharisees kept asking Jesus about the sins of the woman and finally stood up and answered, "Let him who is without sin among you be the first to throw a stone at her." In my opinion, the actions of Jesus inspired me to believe that He didn't answer right away because He was inclining his ear to God to seek how to respond to the Pharisees. Silence gives you the opportunity to hear God and also to ask God how you should respond. I also learned that I most definitely don't have to answer foolishness, but we will discuss that later in this book. The main concept is it takes strength to be silent when you are being tried by the enemy or accused of something which is not true. So, don't think silence is a weakness and don't think of yourself as being weak either when it's time to be quiet.

Psalms 46:10 (ESV) says, *"Be still and know that I am God."* Sometimes our mouth needs to be still and even our thoughts. While you are being still, you will know who God is. If you refuse to be quiet and still, you may miss the opportunity to know Him. You may make the situation worse than it already is. You may cause more harm to yourself or the other person. You may feel like you are winning when you open your mouth to say that hurtful or defensive statement, but you won't be winning at all. And God most definitely can't fight a battle for you if you doing all the talking instead of letting God talk for you.

Your Daily Exercises

Exchange of Thoughts: *This exercise is for you to swap out your negative thoughts for what God thinks of you.*

What thought(s) are you having when you actually say something you shouldn't have said instead of being silent?

Your thought:

God's thought:

A Proclamation to Self: *This exercise is for you to proclaim or make a bold statement to remind yourself that the battle is not yours, but it's the Lord's.*

(Your name), you are....

_____.

Write It Down and See It: *This exercise is for you to hide the Word in your heart through memorization.*
  (1) *First, find the scripture below and fill in the blanks.*
  (2) *Second, write one word, phrase, or sentence from the verse that prophesy or stand out to you.*
  (3) *Third, write that one word, phrase, or sentence on your mirror in the bathroom, in your journal, on a sticky note, or in your cell phone to remember or refer back to it.*

Exodus 14:14 (ESV)
One verse: *"The Lord will _____ for you, and you have only to be _____."*

One word, phrase, or sentence:

_____

It's time to Talk: *This exercise is for you to enjoy talking to God anywhere and anytime about anything that is on your mind. You are welcome to write your prayer on the lines provided below. Keep these five key points in mind when talking to God:*
  1. *Acknowledge Him and tell Him who He is to you.*
  2. *Ask Him to forgive you for any shortcomings in your life.*
  3. *Give Him thanks for everything including the things that may be difficult or a struggle in your life.*
  4. *Tell Him what you need, ask Him freely, and believe that He will give it to you. Because after all, you are His child.*

5. *Seal it, stamp it, and declare it in His Son, Jesus's name!*

_____

_____

_____

_____

_____

_____

_____

_____

_____

_____

Day 10

Anger is not necessary

*"My dear brothers and sisters, take note of this: Everyone should be, slow to speak and **SLOW TO BECOME ANGRY**."* James 1:19 (NIV)

ANGER IS THE most wasteful and dangerous emotional response anyone could ever have, because it tends to be a hazard to your physical, spiritual, social, and mental health. Have you ever got so mad, you got a headache? During that headache, you felt your blood flowing rapidly in your body and your eyes became red even watery. Your body goes through a drastic change when responding to something in anger. Your mind becomes cloudy and disoriented. Next thing you know you may have high blood pressure, stress, and some other kind of sickness. Anger is unnecessary. There's no reason to get upset when people are talking about you. Let them talk. Talk is cheap but your health is expensive. It's expensive and important. It's hard to enjoy life when you are angry. Anger makes you unsatisfied and complain about everything.

To encourage you, allow me to tell you why anger isn't necessary. Psalms 110:1 (ESV) says, *"The Lord says to my Lord, Sit at my right hand until I make your enemies your footstool."* Surely, this is what God said to Jesus, but this is also what He is saying to you. Ephesians 2:5-6 (ESV) says, *"But God, being rich in mercy, because of the great love with which He loved us, even when we were dead in our trespasses, made us alive together with Christ – by grace you have been saved – and raised us up with Him and seated us with Him in the heavenly places in Christ Jesus."* In other words, where Jesus is, so are you. In the heavenly places at the throne sitting by the Lord resting and waiting on God to make your enemies your footstool. Rest again, I say, rest in the fact that God will make it known to your enemies who you are to Him. Psalms 23:5 (NIV) says, *"You prepare a table before me in the presence of my enemies; You anoint my head with oil; my cup overflows."* He will bless you in front of your enemies and let it run over so your enemies will know it is God fighting for you! Getting angry is unnecessary because God has your back and your front. You should keep a mental picture of the throne. Visualize yourself at the throne sitting next to God with your feet propped up waiting for God to wipe out the schemes of your enemy.

Anger has one motive; and that is to destroy. Anger destroys relationships, the body, mind, and soul. In Genesis the 4th chapter (NIV), Cain was angry for numerous reasons. Cain believed his offering wasn't good enough for God. He believed his brother, Abel, was getting all the attention and good report from God. As a result, instead of putting more effort into his own offering for God, he killed Abel out of envy. So, as you can see it started with anger, then envy, and then murder. Anger leads to other sins and if it consumes you, it will lead you to a road of destruction. As James, Chapter 1, verse 20 (NIV) says, *"Because human anger does not produce the righteousness that God desires."*

Allow me to share with you a few ways to calm your anger.

1. Pray. Ask God to give you strength to resist.
2. Sing or listen to your favorite gospel song.
3. Count from 20 to 1.
4. Say your favorite scripture or proclamation.
5. REPEAT, if needed.

Your Daily Exercises

Exchange of Thoughts: *This exercise is for you to swap out your negative thoughts for what God thinks of you.*

What thought(s) are you having when you are angry with someone?

Your thought:

God's thought:

A Proclamation to Self: *This exercise is for you to proclaim or make a bold statement to remind yourself that anger is unnecessary.*

(Your name), you are....

_____.

Write It Down and See It: *This exercise is for you to hide the Word in your heart through memorization.*
   (1) *First, find the scripture below and fill in the blanks.*
   (2) *Second, write one word, phrase, or sentence from the verse that prophesy or stand out to you.*
   (3) *Third, write that one word, phrase, or sentence on your mirror in the bathroom, in your journal, on a sticky note, or in your cell phone to remember or refer back to it.*

James 1:20 (ESV)
One verse: *"For the anger of man _____ _____ produce the righteousness of God."*

One word, phrase, or sentence:

_____

It's time to Talk: *This exercise is for you to enjoy talking to God anywhere and anytime about anything that is on your mind. You are welcome to write your prayer on the lines provided below. Keep these five key points in mind when talking to God:*

1. *Acknowledge Him and tell Him who He is to you.*
2. *Ask Him to forgive you for any shortcomings in your life.*
3. *Give Him thanks for everything including the things that may be difficult or a struggle in your life.*
4. *Tell Him what you need, ask Him freely, and believe that He will give it to you. Because after all, you are His child.*
5. *Seal it, stamp it, and declare it in His Son, Jesus's name!*

_____

_____

_____

_____

_____

_____

_____

_____

_____

_____

_____

Day 11

No Response is a Good Response

"Do not answer a fool according to his folly, or you yourself will be just like him." Proverbs 26:4 (NIV)

BE WISE IN responding to foolishness. No response can be a good response. Everything posted and said in the media does not need a response. Why become foolish just because someone else is acting foolish? You know that person is a fool; and yet you will entertain the fool. Just remember though, when you take the energy and effort to entertain a fool with folly, you are just as foolish as the fool.

Every statement or comment does not need a response. Paul said in First Corinthians 6:12 (NIV), *"All things are lawful for me, but not all things are helpful. All things are lawful for me, but I will not be dominated by anything."* In other words, you can do what you want to do, but everything you do is not helpful or beneficial. It's good to know you have the choice to do what you please, but why be dominated by anything. Why be in bondage to what someone says about you? Why carry on in pity just because someone doesn't like you. Guess what? They didn't like Jesus either, but that didn't stop Him from doing what God had called Him to do. It's not beneficial to you to allow statements or comments to dominate your day. Make a choice to not respond to foolish things. It's okay to erase, delete, block, and repeat!

Social media has a way to make someone be so insecure and inferior, because this is the type of world we live in. A world with cynicism about every little thing. It doesn't have to affect you. You have the authority to block cynicism on your social networks or around you in person. You have the authority, not them! Remember, you can erase, delete, block, and repeat. Also, remember no response is a good response.

"Even a fool who keeps silent is considered wise; when he closes his lips, he is deemed intelligent." Proverbs 17:28 (ESV)

Allow me to share with you ways to give an answer when you don't want to answer foolishness in person.

1. Pray. Ask God to give you strength to resist.
2. I have no comment.
3. I'm speechless.
4. I have no response to what you just said. If asked why. You can say it again that you have no comment.
5. Walk away, if possible.

Allow me to share with you ways to give an answer when you don't want to answer foolishness on social media networks.

1. Pray. Ask God to give you strength to resist.
2. Scroll on.
3. Delete the comment.
4. Block the person.
5. If what was said hurt you, grab your Bible. Read your favorite scripture. Say your proclamations out loud. Say it again, if needed.
6. If that doesn't work, pray.
7. REPEAT.

Your Daily Exercises

Exchange of Thoughts: *This exercise is for you to swap out your negative thoughts for what God thinks of you.*

What thought(s) are you having when you answer foolishness and the foolishness doesn't stop?

Your thought:

God's thought:

A Proclamation to Self: *This exercise is for you to proclaim or make a bold statement to remind yourself that no response can be a good response.*

(Your name), you are....

_____.

Write It Down and See It: *This exercise is for you to hide the Word in your heart through memorization.*
   (1) *First, find the scripture below and fill in the blanks.*
   (2) *Second, write one word, phrase, or sentence from the verse that prophesy or stand out to you.*
   (3) *Third, write that one word, phrase, or sentence on your mirror in the bathroom, in your journal, on a sticky note, or in your cell phone to remember or refer back to it.*

Proverbs 4:11 (NIV)
One verse: *"As a dog returns to its vomit, so _____ repeat their folly."*

One word, phrase, or sentence:

_____

It's time to Talk: *This exercise is for you to enjoy talking to God anywhere and anytime about anything that is on your mind. You are welcome to write your prayer on the lines provided below. Keep these five key points in mind when talking to God:*

1. *Acknowledge Him and tell Him who He is to you.*
2. *Ask Him to forgive you for any shortcomings in your life.*
3. *Give Him thanks for everything including the things that may be difficult or a struggle in your life.*
4. *Tell Him what you need, ask Him freely, and believe that He will give it to you. Because after all, you are His child.*
5. *Seal it, stamp it, and declare it in His Son, Jesus's name!*

_____

_____

_____

_____

_____

_____

_____

_____

_____

Day 12

Answer with Wisdom

"Answer a fool according to his folly, or he will be wise in his own eyes." Proverbs 26:5 (NIV)

IF YOU MUST answer a fool, respond with words or actions so the fool will have learned wisdom. *There's a time for everything under the heaven.* (Ecclesiastes 3:1) The day before was about not responding. This day is about knowing when and what to respond. If you don't want to be foolish in your response, you must seek wisdom. James 1:5 (NIV) says, *"If any of you lacks wisdom, you should ask God, who gives generously to all without finding fault, and it will be given to you."*

God wants you to be wise in your actions. He has no objection to giving you wisdom. Believe it is given to you when you ask for it. When it is given, use it for the edification of God's people. Use it to lift up one another. Use it to prosper and bring good tidings to others as well as yourself. Use it to be generous to someone else who is normally not being treated with generosity. Use it to shame the devil and not others. This war is not against flesh and blood. It's against the devil whose only purpose in life is to kill, steal, and destroy what we allow him to have. You have the authority to be wise in your actions. You have a free will to reign with wisdom and not foolishness. If you must answer a fool, answer with wisdom.

On Day 9, I shared the story about the woman caught in adultery. The Pharisees thought it was beneficial to make a mockery of Jesus knowing the Law of Moses as if He didn't already know the Word. When Jesus was asked the question about what does he think about the woman being stoned for being caught in adultery for it was written in the Law of Moses? Jesus didn't answer quickly, but when He did; He answered with wisdom. The kind of wisdom that blocked the devil from going any further with his schemes. The kind of wisdom that made the people walk away instead of Jesus walking away from the scene. The kind of wisdom that made a way for another soul (the woman caught in adultery) to get it right with God. If you must answer foolishness, answer with this kind of wisdom. If you don't have this kind of wisdom, read the scripture below.

"If any of you lacks wisdom, you should ask God who gives generously to all without finding fault, and it will be given to you." James 1:5 (NIV)

Allow me to share with you ways to begin giving an answer when you can no longer hold your tongue in person.

1. Pray. Ask God for the words to say.
2. I don't mean any disrespect, but I ....
3. You have a right to your opinion. I also have a right to......
4. Let me make sure I am hearing you correctly. Did you just say......?

Allow me to share with you ways to give an answer when you can no longer hold your tongue on social media networks.

1. Pray. Ask God for the words to say.
2. Type slowly.
3. Read over what you typed.
4. Check for typos and foolishness.
5. If what you wrote is meant to hurt or offend, erase it. Start over.
6. If what you wrote the second time still is meant to hurt or offend, erase it, grab your Bible. Read your favorite scripture. Say your proclamations out loud. Say it again, if needed.

7. If that doesn't work, pray.
8. REPEAT.

Your Daily Exercises

Exchange of Thoughts: *This exercise is for you to swap out your negative thoughts for what God thinks of you.*

What thought(s) are you having when God gives you the words to speak when answering foolishness and you don't say it?

Your thought:

God's thought:

A Proclamation to Self: *This exercise is for you to proclaim or make a bold statement to remind yourself that you can seek wisdom from God.*

(Your name), you are....

_____.

Write It Down and See It: *This exercise is for you to hide the Word in your heart through memorization.*
   (1) *First, find the scripture below and fill in the blanks.*
   (2) *Second, write one word, phrase, or sentence from the verse that prophesy or stand out to you.*
   (3) *Third, write that one word, phrase, or sentence on your mirror in the bathroom, in your journal, on a sticky note, or in your cell phone to remember or refer back to it.*

Ephesians 4:29 (NIV)

One verse: *"Do not let unwholesome talk come out of your _____, but only what is helpful for _____ others up according to their needs that it may benefit those who listen."*

One word, phrase, or sentence:

_____

It's time to Talk: *This exercise is for you to enjoy talking to God anywhere and anytime about anything that is on your mind. You are welcome to write your prayer on the lines provided below. Keep these five key points in mind when talking to God:*

1. *Acknowledge Him and tell Him who He is to you.*
2. *Ask Him to forgive you for any shortcomings in your life.*
3. *Give Him thanks for everything including the things that may be difficult or a struggle in your life.*
4. *Tell Him what you need, ask Him freely, and believe that He will give it to you. Because after all, you are His child.*
5. *Seal it, stamp it, and declare it in His Son, Jesus's name!*

_____
_____
_____
_____
_____
_____
_____
_____
_____
_____

Day 13

Be a God-pleaser

"For am I now seeking the approval of man, or of God? Or am I trying to please man? If I were still trying to please man, I would not be a servant of Christ." Galatians 1:10 (ESV)

PAUL MADE A strong statement. If I please man, I will not be a servant of Christ. You can't be both. You are either a God-pleaser or a man-pleaser. God desires you to please Him not man. Answer the following questions, if they apply to you.

    (1) Why do you try so hard to please man?

       _____
       _____

    (2) Why do you wish to have man's approval?

       _____
       _____

    (3) What can man do for you and to you?

       _____
       _____

David said in Psalms 118:6 (ESV), *"The Lord is on my side; I will not fear. What can man do to me? The Lord is on my side as my Helper; I shall look in triumph on those who hate me. It is better to take refuge in the Lord than to trust in man."* Such a strong proclamation from David about not being afraid of man because his refuge is in God. Let this scripture be your proclamation as well when you find yourself pleasing man because you may be afraid of what man may do to you. The Lord is on your side. He is your refuge. He is your Helper. Your purpose on earth is not to please man. Man cannot do anything to you or for you that God does not allow. Be a God-pleaser.

"When a man's ways please the Lord, He makes even his enemies to be at peace with him." Proverbs 16:7 (ESV)

When you please God, your enemies will be at peace with you. Surely, there will be people who don't like you due to the fact that you choose to do what God told you to do. Always remember you are not fighting against flesh and blood, but you are fighting the real culprit, Satan. You can never go wrong pleasing God or being about your Father's business like Jesus did. You can go wrong by pleasing man because man cannot be pleased. Man is never satisfied. There will always be someone who didn't like what you did; didn't like what you said; didn't like what you wore; etc. etc. The only thing that should matter to you is that you do what God told you to do. For He is the One who woke you up this morning. He's the One who blessed you with all the things you have. He's the One who gave you the skills and talents to do what you do. He's the only One who can take it away!

"Do not be afraid of those who kill the body but cannot kill the soul. Rather, be afraid of the One who can destroy both soul and body in hell." Matthew 10:28 (NIV)

Your Daily Exercises

Exchange of Thoughts: *This exercise is for you to swap out your negative thoughts for what God thinks of you.*

What thought(s) are you having when you are pleasing man instead of God?

Your thought:

God's thought:

A Proclamation to Self: *This exercise is for you to proclaim or make a bold statement to remind yourself that pleasing God is better than pleasing man.*

(Your name), you are....

_____.

Write It Down and See It: *This exercise is for you to hide the Word in your heart through memorization.*
   (1) *First, find the scripture below and fill in the blanks.*
   (2) *Second, write one word, phrase, or sentence from the verse that prophesy or stand out to you.*
   (3) *Third, write that one word, phrase, or sentence on your mirror in the bathroom, in your journal, on a sticky note, or in your cell phone to remember or refer back to it.*

Colossians 3:23 (ESV)
One verse: *"Whatever you do, work heartily, as for the _____ and not for man."*

One word, phrase, or sentence:

_____

It's time to Talk: *This exercise is for you to enjoy talking to God anywhere and anytime about anything that is on your mind. You are welcome to write your prayer on the lines provided below. Keep these five key points in mind when talking to God:*

1. *Acknowledge Him and tell Him who He is to you.*
2. *Ask Him to forgive you for any shortcomings in your life.*
3. *Give Him thanks for everything including the things that may be difficult or a struggle in your life.*
4. *Tell Him what you need, ask Him freely, and believe that He will give it to you. Because after all, you are His child.*
5. *Seal it, stamp it, and declare it in His Son, Jesus's name!*

_____

_____

_____

_____

_____

_____

_____

_____

_____

_____

Day 14

Allow their Criticism to be Your Motivation

"Do not be afraid; you will not be put to shame. Do not fear disgrace; you will not be humiliated." Isaiah 54:4a (NIV)

YOU ARE NOT immune from others' criticism about you. People will be cynical to what you choose to do with your life. But even so, let their criticism be your motivation to turn them into liars. It doesn't make sense to fight a person for thinking or believing you won't go far in life or amount to anything. Philippians 1:6 (NIV) says, *"Being confident of this, that He who began a good work in you will carry it on to completion until the day of Christ Jesus."* God already knows the plans He has for you, plans to prosper and not to harm you, plans to give you hope and a future. Jeremiah 29:11 (NIV). All you have to do is believe and have faith in God's Word. Hebrews 11:6 (NIV) says, *"And without faith it is impossible to please God, because anyone who comes to Him must believe that He exists and that He rewards those who earnestly seek Him."*

Beloved, I am asking you to seek Him in regards to your life and what you should be doing in this world to edify God's people and including yourself. Be lifted up and exalt His name for He will always have a heart for you. You are always on His mind. You are important to Him and He wants you to enjoy life to the fullest. Let people talk, because sometimes that is all it is – talk. Even when they plot against you, always remember to declare, *"No weapon that is fashioned against you shall succeed, and you shall refute every tongue that rises against you in judgment. This is the heritage of the servants of the Lord and their vindication from me, declares the Lord."* Isaiah 54:17 (ESV)

Your Daily Exercises

Exchange of Thoughts: *This exercise is for you to swap out your negative thoughts for what God thinks of you.*

What thought(s) are you having when people are criticizing you for what you do or don't do?

Your thought:

God's thought:

A Proclamation to Self: *This exercise is for you to proclaim or make a bold statement to remind yourself that God will not put you to shame.*

(Your name), you are....

_____.

Write It Down and See It: *This exercise is for you to hide the Word in your heart through memorization.*
  (1) *First, find the scripture below and fill in the blanks.*
  (2) *Second, write one word, phrase, or sentence from the verse that prophesy or stand out to you.*

(3) Third, write that one word, phrase, or sentence on your mirror in the bathroom, in your journal, on a sticky note, or in your cell phone to remember or refer back to it.

Psalm 25:2 (NIV)
One verse: *"I trust in You; do not let me be put to _____, nor let my enemies triumph over me."*

One word, phrase, or sentence:

_____

It's time to Talk: *This exercise is for you to enjoy talking to God anywhere and anytime about anything that is on your mind. You are welcome to write your prayer on the lines provided below. Keep these five key points in mind when talking to God:*

1. *Acknowledge Him and tell Him who He is to you.*
2. *Ask Him to forgive you for any shortcomings in your life.*
3. *Give Him thanks for everything including the things that may be difficult or a struggle in your life.*
4. *Tell Him what you need, ask Him freely, and believe that He will give it to you. Because after all, you are His child.*
5. *Seal it, stamp it, and declare it in His Son, Jesus's name!*

_____
_____
_____
_____
_____
_____
_____
_____
_____
_____

Gird your loins with Truth

Day 15

Be Lead in Truth

"God is not man that He should lie; neither the son of man that He should repent; has he said, and shall He not do it? Or Has He spoken, and shall He not make it good? Numbers 23:19 (KJV)

GOD DOES NOT lie and neither does His word come back void. His Word completes what it is sent out to do. Satan is the one who lies. He is actually the father of lies and no truth is in him. He uses lies to steal, kill, and destroy whatever we allow him. It is your responsibility to know the truth. It is not the Pastor's responsibility to make sure you know the Word. Read God's Word for yourself. His Word is truth. *You must gird your loins with truth to stand firm against the wiles of the devil.* (Ephesians 6:14 KJV). You can't stand firm if you are not reading God's Word. The more you read God's Word, the stronger you will become against cynicism in today's society.

"Thy word is a lamp unto my feet and a light unto my path." Psalm 119:105 (KJV)

The Holy Bible is to be used as a guide to conquer the world. The world can be a dark place when you are not prepared to conquer it. You will need guidance through the night and through the day. The Holy Bible is not to be used as a contest on who can quote the most scriptures, who can read the most books in one day, or who can find the scripture without looking in the concordance. By the way, that's the purpose of the concordance and table of contents; so you can find what you need to conquer any issues in your life. Know your truth which is collided with God's truth. Know who you are in Christ. Know whose you are and what you are capable of with the love of Christ. Be guided with truth.

Don't be afraid to speak your truth, either. The truth which is collided with God's truth. The Word is written to be repeated and resounded in the atmosphere. God says His word does not come back void and it will accomplish that which He purposed. (Isaiah 55:11 ESV) So, speak His word to do what it is purposed to do. For an example: if you are in the midst of a situation that you have no control to change and you need peace, you can speak the truth about obtaining peace from many scriptures in the Bible. My favorite scripture to speak in the atmosphere when I need peace is, *"You keep him in perfect peace whose mind is stayed on you, because he trusts in you."* Isaiah 26:3 (ESV). What I do is take this scripture and make it personal: *Lord, Your Word says You will keep me in perfect peace when my mind is stayed on you and because I trust in you.* Don't just read His Word, make it personal. Make it a habit. Make it a day to day job.

The purpose of speaking scripture out loud or in the atmosphere is to shift a change in you. It is our human nature to want our situation to change quickly, but let's be realistic, some things are not done quickly just because we pray, fast, go to church three times a week, and/or read the bible. A shifting can take place, but it starts in you. You can change the course of action or events in your life by first changing you. It may be scary, frightening, or hard to accomplish due to wanting to stay in our comfort zone. Believe me, I know it well. God would not be God if He allows us to stay in our zone of comfort or should I say, *mess.*

Your Daily Exercises

Exchange of Thoughts: *This exercise is for you to swap out your negative thoughts for what God thinks of you.*

What thought(s) are you having when you speak God's Word and nothing happens to your situation?

Your thought:

God's thought:

A Proclamation to Self: *This exercise is for you to proclaim or make a bold statement to remind yourself that the change begins with you first.*

(Your name), you are....

_____.

Write It Down and See It: *This exercise is for you to hide the Word in your heart through memorization.*
   (1) *First, find the scripture below and fill in the blanks.*
   (2) *Second, write one word, phrase, or sentence from the verse that prophesy or stand out to you.*
   (3) *Third, write that one word, phrase, or sentence on your mirror in the bathroom, in your journal, on a sticky note, or in your cell phone to remember or refer back to it.*

Exodus 14:14 (ESV)
One verse: *"Lead me in _____ and teach me, for you are the God of my salvation; for you I wait all the day long."* Psalm 25:5 (ESV)

One word, phrase, or sentence:
_____

It's time to Talk: *This exercise is for you to enjoy talking to God anywhere and anytime about anything that is on your mind. You are* welcome to write your prayer on the lines provided below. Keep these five key points in mind when talking to God:

1. Acknowledge Him and tell Him who He is to you.
2. Ask Him to forgive you for any shortcomings in your life.
3. Give Him thanks for everything including the things that may be difficult or a struggle in your life.
4. Tell Him what you need, ask Him freely, and believe that He will give it to you. Because after all, you are His child.
5. Seal it, stamp it, and declare it in His Son, Jesus's name!

_____

_____

_____

_____

_____

_____

_____

_____

_____

_____

Day 16

Speak Well of Yourself & Others

"Death and life are in the power of the tongue, and those who love it will eat its fruits." Proverbs 18:21 (ESV)

OUR WORDS HOLD power. Power to hurt or to heal. Power to tear down or to build up. Power to deliver or to bind. Power to restore or to damage. It is you who choose the course of action you wish to give to either yourself or others. It is imperative for you to speak well of yourself as well as others. Whichever you love, you will eat the fruit thereof. If you love to gossip, talk about people, say blunt, hurtful things to people, you will reap the fruit thereof.

"Do not be deceived: God is not mocked, for whatever one sows that will he also reap. For the one who sows to his own flesh will from the flesh reap corruption, but the one who sows to the Spirit will from the Spirit reap eternal life." Galatians 6:7-8 (ESV)

There's nothing good you could ever reap for tearing down another person or yourself. You will reap bitterness, unkindness, dissatisfaction, and malice in your heart. If you speak words that build up, heal, restore, and deliver, you will reap contentment, love, compassion, and peace in your heart. God didn't create you to put yourself or others down. He created you to build up and be a light unto others. Speak well of yourself and you will reap the benefits of building up yourself. Speak well of others and you will reap the benefits of building up God's people. Love yourself well and you will reap the benefits of love. Love others well and they will reap the benefits of love. You hold the power in your tongue. Let your words fall with grace and compassion when you speak.

Let's talk about the times when you don't have anything nice to say. If you don't have anything nice to say, be quiet. Remember, no response is a good response. If people are always coming to you to talk about others, you may want to check yourself. What is it about you that make others so comfortable to talk about other people to you? What are you doing about it to make sure that doesn't happen again? Do you like it when others are tearing down other people? Do you like it when you tear down other people? Do you like to slander and gossip? These are good questions to reflect in your private time with God. You can change the habit of gossiping and slander. You have to seek His face and ask for strategies to use to conquer these issues. *You can do all things through the strength of Christ.* (Philippians 4:13) You cannot do it alone.

Your Daily Exercises

Exchange of Thoughts: *This exercise is for you to swap out your negative thoughts for what God thinks of you.*

What thought(s) are you having when you are saying negative things about yourself or others?

Your thought:

God's thought:

A Proclamation to Self: *This exercise is for you to proclaim or make a bold statement to remind yourself that that you should speak well of yourself and others.*

(Your name), you are....

_____.

Write It Down and See It: *This exercise is for you to hide the Word in your heart through memorization.*
   (1) *First, find the scripture below and fill in the blanks.*
   (2) *Second, write one word, phrase, or sentence from the verse that prophesy or stand out to you.*
   (3) *Third, write that one word, phrase, or sentence on your mirror in the bathroom, in your journal, on a sticky note, or in your cell phone to remember or refer back to it.*

Proverbs 15:4 (ESV)
One verse: *"A gentle tongue is a tree of* _____, *but perverseness in it breaks the* _____*."*

One word, phrase, or sentence:

_____

It's time to Talk: *This exercise is for you to enjoy talking to God anywhere and anytime about anything that is on your mind. You are welcome to write your prayer on the lines provided below. Keep these five key points in mind when talking to God:*
   1. *Acknowledge Him and tell Him who He is to you.*
   2. *Ask Him to forgive you for any shortcomings in your life.*
   3. *Give Him thanks for everything including the things that may be difficult or a struggle in your life.*
   4. *Tell Him what you need, ask Him freely, and believe that He will give it to you. Because after all, you are His child.*
   5. *Seal it, stamp it, and declare it in His Son, Jesus's name!*

_____

_____

_____

_____

_____

_____

_____

_____

_____

_____

Day 17

Be Accountable for Your Actions

"So then each of us will give an account of himself to God." Romans 14:12 (ESV)

BE ACCOUNTABLE FOR your own actions. If you react a certain way that is outside the will of God, it is solely your fault. It is not the devil. It is not your family. It is not your church family. It is not the other person. It is you! You are responsible for your own actions. Own up to it. Be truthful about it. Remember to gird your loins with truth. God despises liars. He hold us all accountable for our own actions, feelings, and thoughts. Philippians 2:12 (KJV) says, *"Work out your own salvation with fear and trembling."*

The blaming game may have started when Adam blamed Eve for eating the forbidden fruit, but Jesus abolished the blaming game when he died for our sins. You can no longer use the defense of blaming others for your own choice of words, actions that are out of your character, and judgment of reactions to extenuating circumstances. Don't be afraid to be accountable for what you do. Man does not have a heaven or hell to put you in, but God does. If you don't know how to be accountable, ask God for guidance. He can help you choose your words and actions wisely. You are not capable of fulfilling this task alone. You need the Holy Spirit to guide and strengthen you to do the righteous thing in the eyes of God. *It is God who works in you to will and to act in order to fulfill His good purpose.* (Philippians 2:13 NIV).

I have five children and ever since they were of an age of knowing right from wrong, I taught them how to be accountable for their own actions. I hated with a passion when they lied about what they did, especially when I knew they were lying. Instead of showing my anger, I would show my sweet side to coerce them into telling the truth. I would assure them if they told the truth, I wouldn't punish them. I meant it, too. When I asked them why they did what they did, they would respond, *"I don't know."* (This is the second thing I hated with a passion.) So, I would respond, *"Yes, you do know. You did it because you wanted to do it. Not because you were coerced to do it. You did it because you wanted to do it. Now say it!"* Then, they would say they did it because they wanted to do it. I would also ask them what they should do next time when that situation arises. I would offer strategies on what to do next time or they will have to answer to me. I share this to say three things:

(1.) Being accountable is to not lie.

(2.) Being accountable is to own the actions by admitting you did it, because you wanted to do it.

(3.) Being accountable is to learn from the situation by implementing strategies to not do it again.

Your Daily Exercises

Exchange of Thoughts: *This exercise is for you to swap out your negative thoughts for what God thinks of you.*

What thought(s) are you having when you don't want to be accountable for your own actions, especially when the other person had a part in the matter?

Your thought:

God's thought:

A Proclamation to Self: *This exercise is for you to proclaim or make a bold statement to remind yourself that you will be held accountable for everything you do on Judgment Day.*

(Your name), you are....

_____.

Write It Down and See It: *This exercise is for you to hide the Word in your heart through memorization.*
    (1) *First, find the scripture below and fill in the blanks.*
    (2) *Second, write one word, phrase, or sentence from the verse that prophesy or stand out to you.*
    (3) *Third, write that one word, phrase, or sentence on your mirror in the bathroom, in your journal, on a sticky note, or in your cell phone to remember or refer back to it.*

Psalms 86:11 (ESV)
One verse: *"Teach me _____ O' Lord, that I may _____ in your truth; unite my heart to fear your name."*

One word, phrase, or sentence:
_____

It's time to Talk: *This exercise is for you to enjoy talking to God anywhere and anytime about anything that is on your mind. You are welcome to write your prayer on the lines provided below. Keep these five key points in mind when talking to God:*
    1. *Acknowledge Him and tell Him who He is to you.*
    2. *Ask Him to forgive you for any shortcomings in your life.*
    3. *Give Him thanks for everything including the things that may be difficult or a struggle in your life.*

4. *Tell Him what you need, ask Him freely, and believe that He will give it to you. Because after all, you are His child.*
5. *Seal it, stamp it, and declare it in His Son, Jesus's name!*

_____

_____

_____

_____

_____

_____

_____

_____

_____

_____

Day 18
Choose Life not Death

"I call heaven and earth to witness against you today, that I have set before you life and death, blessing and curse. Therefore choose life, that you and your offspring may live." Deuteronomy 30:19 (ESV)

TO CHOOSE IS freedom. You have the right to live your life however you choose to live it. Others have the right to live their lives however they choose to live it. You are not responsible for others choose to live their lives. God desires everyone to choose life not death. The choice *is* absolutely yours. Always remember that when you see someone else living recklessly. The choice *is* absolutely theirs. God is not a God who will make you love Him. He would rather have you make your own decision to love Him or not. When you love Him, you will love His commandments and paths He has already ordained for you to follow. You are free to live a victorious or defeated life. You are free to live or die. You are free to be happy or sad. You are free to be cautious or reckless. You are free to do and say as you please. Remember, you will reap the fruit thereof. Also, your offspring will reap the fruit thereof.

God is so mindful of His children that He sent His only begotten Son to save us from our wickedness. You have no reason to be self-destructive. Surely, bad things can happen to you just like it can happen to anyone, but it is not healthy to be self-destructive. It is not even healthy for your love ones who care about you. If sin is reigning in your life and hindering your divine purpose, all you have to do is make a <u>choice</u> to not sin anymore. Make a choice to have no more death to your purpose, ministry, finances, conversations, etc. Bring forth life, dear! Be bold and walk in knowing whose you are so you may have life!

In the fourth chapter of John, Jesus was at the well when a Samaritan woman came to draw water. He asked her for a drink of water. They continued their conversation about living water which Jesus knew the Samaritan woman needed. The point I want to bring from the fourth chapter is when Jesus asked the woman to go get her husband. She answered saying that she had no husband. Jesus told her she was right. She had five husbands and the one she was with at the time was not her husband. The first question that came to my mind was, *"what need did this woman want met that she had to be with many men trying to obtain?"*

I knew the answer well for I was seeking the same thing when I was young. I wanted to be loved. I was thirsty for acceptance. I longed to be a wife. I was self-destructive and laying down my soul not knowing all I needed was the living water Jesus could provide for eternity. When I came to myself, I did make a choice to give my life to Christ. I wanted to live and not die being miserable. It is possible to be whole again. It is possible to be free. It is possible to be happy. I know it well. I pray you do, too.

Your Daily Exercises

Exchange of Thoughts: *This exercise is for you to swap out your negative thoughts for what God thinks of you.*

What thought(s) are you having when you feel like you are just going through the motion or stuck in the wilderness roaming with no life of fresh air?

Your thought:

God's thought:

A Proclamation to Self: *This exercise is for you to proclaim or make a bold statement to remind yourself God wants the best for you.*

(Your name), you are....

_____.

Write It Down and See It: *This exercise is for you to hide the Word in your heart through memorization.*
  (1) *First, find the scripture below and fill in the blanks.*
  (2) *Second, write one word, phrase, or sentence from the verse that prophesy or stand out to you.*
  (3) *Third, write that one word, phrase, or sentence on your mirror in the bathroom, in your journal, on a sticky note, or in your cell phone to remember or refer back to it.*

Psalms 118:17 (ESV)
One verse: *"I shall not _____, but I shall _____, and recount the deeds of the Lord."*

One word, phrase, or sentence:

_____

It's time to Talk: *This exercise is for you to enjoy talking to God anywhere and anytime about anything that is on your mind. You are welcome to write your prayer on the lines provided below. Keep these five key points in mind when talking to God:*
  1. *Acknowledge Him and tell Him who He is to you.*
  2. *Ask Him to forgive you for any shortcomings in your life.*
  3. *Give Him thanks for everything including the things that may be difficult or a struggle in your life.*
  4. *Tell Him what you need, ask Him freely, and believe that He will give it to you. Because after all, you are His child.*

5. *Seal it, stamp it, and declare it in His Son, Jesus's name!*

_____
_____
_____
_____
_____
_____
_____
_____
_____
_____

Day 19

Be Yourself without Apology

"But by the grace of God I am what I am, and His grace toward me was not in vain. On the contrary I worked harder than any of them, though it was not I, but the grace of God that is in me." 1 Corinthians 15:10 (ESV)

YOU OWE NO apology for what God has designed you to be. You owe no apology for the gifts He has bestowed upon you to make room for you and be seated among great men. You owe no apology for the anointing He has poured upon your head to operate in the gifts God has given you. You owe no apology for working hard in excellence for the Lord. You owe no apology for fulfilling the calling He has ordained you to do. You owe no apology. Be who God has designed you to be. Whether you stutter or not, physically challenged or not, educated with a degree or not. Be who God has ordained you to be. It is not by accident you were made the way you are. It is not by accident you speak the way you do. It is not by accident you walk the way you walk. God makes no mistakes in creating what He desires and calls to be good. Stop apologizing to people for being who you are.

The other thing humans like to do is compare themselves to others. Comparing yourself to other people is like telling God you don't appreciate how He created you. God didn't create us to compare ourselves with others. Remember, we are to build each other up not tear each other down. We have no reason to be envious, because we all have something unique to contribute to society. Cain may not have killed Abel if he had not been comparing his offering to Abel's offering. (Genesis 4) Esther would not have been Queen if she did compared herself to the other virgins who were summoned to meet King Ahasuerus. (Esther 2) We all have something to contribute and Satan knows it well. So, he uses this tactic to get you distracted from doing God's will. Comparing yourself to others will paralyze your purpose and make you focus on what you need to improve. If there's anything to improve, it's to improve your love for God's will. Compare not yourself to others. It's a lost cause.

You were predestined to fulfill your purpose in this cynical society. You have no control over what others say about you, but you do have control over what you do. You only need God's stamp of approval and favor. Ask yourself the following questions when you find yourself doubting who you are:

(1) What is God saying to you?
(2) What is God telling you to do?
(3) Am I seeking God's approval or man's approval?

Your Daily Exercises

Exchange of Thoughts: *This exercise is for you to swap out your negative thoughts for what God thinks of you.*

What thought(s) are you having when people are telling you to change your looks or the way you do things?

Your thought:

God's thought:

A Proclamation to Self: *This exercise is for you to proclaim or make a bold statement to remind yourself that God created you not man.*

(Your name), you are....

_____.

Write It Down and See It: *This exercise is for you to hide the Word in your heart through memorization.*
  (1) *First, find the scripture below and fill in the blanks.*
  (2) *Second, write one word, phrase, or sentence from the verse that prophesy or stand out to you.*
  (3) *Third, write that one word, phrase, or sentence on your mirror in the bathroom, in your journal, on a sticky note, or in your cell phone to remember or refer back to it.*

Psalms 139:13 (ESV)
One verse: *"For you formed my _____ parts; you knitted me together in my mother's womb."*

One word, phrase, or sentence:

_____

It's time to Talk: *This exercise is for you to enjoy talking to God anywhere and anytime about anything that is on your mind. You are welcome to write your prayer on the lines provided below. Keep these five key points in mind when talking to God:*
  1. *Acknowledge Him and tell Him who He is to you.*
  2. *Ask Him to forgive you for any shortcomings in your life.*
  3. *Give Him thanks for everything including the things that may be difficult or a struggle in your life.*
  4. *Tell Him what you need, ask Him freely, and believe that He will give it to you. Because after all, you are His child.*
  5. *Seal it, stamp it, and declare it in His Son, Jesus's name!*

_____
_____

Day 20
Silence Your Thoughts

"For though we walk in the flesh, we are not waging war according to the flesh. For the weapons of our warfare are not of the flesh but have divine power to destroy strongholds. We destroy arguments and every lofty opinion raised against the knowledge of God and take every though captive to obey Christ." 2 Corinthians 10:3-5 (ESV)

THE KEY TO casting down or silencing the negative and deceitful thoughts is to counterattack with a scripture. The only way to counterattack is to speak a specific scripture for the specific attack without hesitation and doubt. For example, when Jesus was tempted by Satan in the wilderness after 40 days and nights of fasting, He spoke a scripture for every temptation Satan brought to Him. (Matthew 4:1-11) You can use the same strategy for every dead thought, every deceitful lie told against you, and every negative thought you may have against yourself.

In the scripture above, Paul says the weapons of our warfare have divine power to destroy strongholds. That weapon is God's Word. There's a scripture in the Holy Bible for every situation that may come upon your life. You have to spend time memorizing the Word that fits your battle. You can tear down what needs to be torn down. You can destroy arguments and every opinion through His Word. You can resist the devil by speaking God's Word and believe that Word will fulfill what it is set out to do. *You* are not fighting flesh and blood. You are fighting against principalities and spiritual forces of evil in the heavenly places. (Ephesians 6:12) God has given you the proper uniform (Armor of God) to wear daily to stand against the schemes of the devil. The belt of truth, breastplate of righteousness, shoes of peace, shield of faith which will put out all the schemes of the devil, helmet of salvation, and the sword of the Spirit which is the Word of God. Prayer is the key to set this uniform in motion to fight your spiritual battles with victory! Don't ever go into battle without praying first. To battle without praying first is like getting in the car without the keys. Your car will sit idly without power until you get the keys to ignite the engine. Put your armor on daily with the intention to tear down strongholds of the mind, body, and spirit. Proclaim your victory! Be like David when He told Goliath that God was going to deliver him into his hands! Be not afraid, because God is with you!

Allow me to share with you ways to silence your thoughts or tear down strongholds.

1. Pray.
2. Seek the right scripture for the specific issue you want to destroy.
3. Read the scripture aloud.
4. Believe the Word will perform what it is set out to do.
5. When you get those negative or distracting thoughts, play your favorite gospel music. Sing along with it. Turn it up if needed.
6. REPEAT, if needed.

Your Daily Exercises

Exchange of Thoughts: *This exercise is for you to swap out your negative thoughts for what God thinks of you.*

What thought(s) are you having when you want to use the scripture to fight, but the first thing you do is speak your fleshly mind?

Your thought:

God's thought:

A Proclamation to Self: *This exercise is for you to proclaim or make a bold statement to remind yourself that you need God's Word to fight the enemy which is not flesh and blood.*

(Your name), you are....

_____.

Write It Down and See It: *This exercise is for you to hide the Word in your heart through memorization.*
   (1) First, find the scripture below and fill in the blanks.
   (2) Second, write one word, phrase, or sentence from the verse that prophesy or stand out to you.
   (3) Third, write that one word, phrase, or sentence on your mirror in the bathroom, in your journal, on a sticky note, or in your cell phone to remember or refer back to it.

Psalms 119:11 (NIV)
One verse: *"I have hidden _____ in my heart that I might not sin against you."*

One word, phrase, or sentence:

_____

It's time to Talk: *This exercise is for you to enjoy talking to God anywhere and anytime about anything that is on your mind. You are welcome to write your prayer on the lines provided below. Keep these five key points in mind when talking to God:*
   1. Acknowledge Him and tell Him who He is to you.
   2. Ask Him to forgive you for any shortcomings in your life.

3. Give Him thanks for everything including the things that may be difficult or a struggle in your life.
4. Tell Him what you need, ask Him freely, and believe that He will give it to you. Because after all, you are His child.
5. Seal it, stamp it, and declare it in His Son, Jesus's name!

_____

_____

_____

_____

_____

_____

_____

_____

_____

Day 21

Think on These Things

"Finally, brethren, whatsoever things are true, whatsoever things are honest, whatsoever things are just, whatsoever things are pure, whatsoever things are lovely, whatsoever things are of good report; if there be any virtue, and if there be any praise, think on these things."
Philippians 4:8 (KJV)

SIMPLY TOLD IN a plain language to think on things that are true, honest, just, pure, lovely, and of good report. If there be any praise, think on these things. You wouldn't have the energy to answer every negative opinion of you or cynicism, if you think on these things. You wouldn't have the energy to compare yourself to others, if you think on these things. You wouldn't have the energy to apologize for being *"the* you" God created you to be, if you think on these things. You wouldn't have the energy to be discontent and angry at yourself, if you think on these things. These things are from above and need to be shared with others. Let heaven reign on earth by sharing good thoughts and feelings that are of God. You don't have to dwell on anything you choose not to dwell on. Put forth more energy on the positive than the negative. Negativity attracts negativity and positivity attracts positivity. If you need positive energy to encompass you, then you must first reflect positivity. Prayerfully, the ones who don't like your positivity will move on to another vessel of space to invade. Apologize? Not for being positive!

Your Daily Exercises

Exchange of Thoughts: *This exercise is for you to swap out your negative thoughts for what God thinks of you.*

What thought(s) are you having when you are not thinking on things that are pure, lovely, good, just, honest, and of good report?

Your thought:

God's thought:

A Proclamation to Self: *This exercise is for you to proclaim or make a bold statement to remind yourself of the good things in life.*

(Your name), you are....

_____.

Write It Down and See It: *This exercise is for you to hide the Word in your heart through memorization.*
   (1) *First, find the scripture below and fill in the blanks.*
   (2) *Second, write one word, phrase, or sentence from the verse that prophesy or stand out to you.*
   (3) *Third, write that one word, phrase, or sentence on your mirror in the bathroom, in your journal, on a sticky note, or in your cell phone to remember or refer back to it.*

Colossians 3:2 (NIV)

One verse: *"Set your minds on _____, not on earthly things."*

One word, phrase, or sentence:

_____

It's time to Talk: *This exercise is for you to enjoy talking to God anywhere and anytime about anything that is on your mind. You are welcome to write your prayer on the lines provided below. Keep these five key points in mind when talking to God:*

1. *Acknowledge Him and tell Him who He is to you.*
2. *Ask Him to forgive you for any shortcomings in your life.*
3. *Give Him thanks for everything including the things that may be difficult or a struggle in your life.*
4. *Tell Him what you need, ask Him freely, and believe that He will give it to you. Because after all, you are His child.*
5. *Seal it, stamp it, and declare it in His Son, Jesus's name!*

_____
_____
_____
_____
_____
_____
_____
_____
_____

Connect with the Author

Website: www.tyrarowell.com
Facebook: www.facebook.com/TyraERowell
Twitter: @TyraRowell
Email: pr@tyrarowell.com

Group Sessions Guide

If you desire to lead a three week group bible study with this book, you can utilize the following group session lessons. You are welcome to complete the contact form on my website to stay tuned on more resources for this book.

Group Session 1

Title: In His Likeness

Icebreaker Activity: (10-15 minutes)

Divide the group members into equal teams of three or four. Each team is to share the following information with the group:

1. Who are you in Christ Jesus?
2. Name one of your strengths and one weakness.
3. What is your God-given gift, task, or talent?

Scripture:

"So God created man in His own image, in the image of God He created him; male and female He created them." Genesis 1:27 (ESV)

Introduction of the Lesson:

Child of God, you are not inadequate, because your Daddy in Heaven is not inadequate. You are a reflection of Him. You were made in His image. When you look in the mirror, you are to smile and admire *who* made you. It isn't beneficial to you to acknowledge all the imperfections and flaws. The mirror should be a tool for you to admire the One who made you. He made you in the likeness of Him. Let's be clear, though. That doesn't mean you have total superior powers like God, but you do have victory already over every situation. You have victory, because you serve a victorious God who you have (prayerfully) given total control over your life. He knew you before your mom and dad even thought to get together. He knows your weaknesses as well as your strengths. There is not a thought you could hide from Him. There's not a wrinkle you could cover up as if He doesn't already know. There's not a bald spot he doesn't already see. He knows you from your head to your toe. He also know your past, present, and future. He knows the decisions you will make in the future. He already knows. So, since He already knows, there's no point in acknowledging your imperfections and flaws. They do not make you less of a man, woman, boy, or girl in His eyesight. Not one bit less!

Discussion/Questions:

In Exodus the third and fourth chapter (NIV), God chose Moses to lead God's people from the oppression of Pharaoh in Egypt. Moses's first reply was, "Who am I to go to Pharaoh and bring the children of Israel out of Egypt?" God replied, "I will be with you and this shall be the sign for you that I have sent you." Moses replied the second time, "If I go to the people telling them the God of their fathers has sent me, and they ask what his name is, what shall I say to them?" God replied to Moses, "I Am who I Am. Say to the children of Israel, I Am has sent me to you." God continued to give Moses more instructions on what to tell His people. He also let Moses know that He already know that Pharaoh is not going to let the children of Israel go until He strike Egypt with wonders and plagues. Moses replied the third time, "They will not believe me?" God gave him instructions on different signs of wonders to use so they will believe him. Moses replied the fourth time, "I am not eloquent. I am slow of speech and slow of tongue." God replied, "Who made man's mouth? Who makes him mute, or deaf, or seeing, or blind? Is it not I, the Lord? Now, go, I will be with your mouth and teach you what you shall speak." Moses replied the fifth time, "Lord, is there someone else you can send?" God got a little angry with Moses, but He gave instructions to Moses that Aaron will be with him and He will used both of their mouths to speak what needs to be said.

Ask the group the following question and allow a few of the members to share their testimony:

Have you ever asked this question of yourself when God gave you a task to complete, *who am I?*

Who are you? You are the one God chose to complete that task He has asked you to do. Whatever He asked of you to do, He has already put in you the things you need to complete it. It's impossible to be inadequate in something God has already placed in you, because what He has placed in you is ordained to perform what it is told to do. You can run from it and decide not to do it. You can even try to talk God out of it like Moses, but you will perform that task God has chosen you to do. The next time you are summoned to complete a task, don't second-guess yourself. Don't feel like you are not adequate enough to do the job. Don't try to talk yourself out of it. God know you and has already equipped you with the gifts, strategies, and resources to complete the task. Don't miss another opportunity to glorify God with what He has already placed in you. You are good enough! Yes, you!

Ask the group the following question and allow a few of the members to share their testimony:

Have you ever tried to explain to God why you shouldn't be the one to complete your God-given task?

Conclusion:

Introduce the outline for the week as well as explain the daily exercises to be completed each day. Leaders, encourage everyone in the study group to complete their daily exercises and offer incentives to get more participation.

Outline for the Week

I.   Be Aware of Whose You Are
II.   You Were Never Created to be Inadequate
III. It is God who Justified You
IV.   You have Access to God
V.   God Is With You
VI.   Surrender to His Love for You
VII. You were Made for Him

Group Session 2

Title: Quench the Lies, not the Spirit

Icebreaker Activity:

Allow one to two members to share one thing they had learned from the daily inspirational. (5 minutes)
Divide the group members into equal teams of three or four. Each team is to share the following information with the group: (10-15 minutes)

1. Have you ever experience criticism that wasn't true?
2. If yes, how did you react to the situation?
3. Did you react the way God desired you to react? If not, how should you have handle the situation?

Scripture:

"My dear brothers and sisters, take note of this: Everyone should be quick to listen, slow to speak and slow to become angry." James 1:19 (NIV)

Introduction of the Lesson:

Being lied on or misunderstood is inevitable. It's going to happen. God is holding you responsible of knowing how to react when things are spoken about you that is not true. So, react by quenching the lies instead of quenching the Spirit. Quench, according to *dictionary.reference.com,* means to put out or extinguish. There are lies being spoken in the atmosphere against you and surely has no merit but to make you doubt God. These type of lies need to be put out like fire or the flame of lies will spread. Lies can take hold of a person's mind by first entering the ears, but once it take hold of the mind it can take root in the heart. Once it's rooted, it will be tended to like it's the absolute truth by being defensive, responding with contempt, and getting angry at times.

Discussion/Questions:

You don't have to believe every word that proceeds out of people's mouths. Especially people who are cynical and love to belittle others. At times, you may hear things about you from people who you may think are not cynical. The Word says, *try the spirit and see if it's of God* (1 John 4:1 KJV). You have to take the time to listen and test the spirit of those who are talking to you. While you are listening you will know if what they are saying or prophesying to you is or not of God. When you are quick to listen instead of responding, it gives you a chance to check in with God. God can hear your thoughts and when you are talking to him, He will give you instructions or strategies on how to respond or react. You quench the lies and not the Spirit by not saying what you really want to say, but saying what God tell you say. What you really want to say may not be the right thing to say.

Ask the group the following questions and allow a few of the members to share their answers: (utilize Biblical scriptures and role-play some reactions)

1. Do you believe you have to respond to everything someone says about you?
2. Name some ways you can react to criticism that hurts, belittles, or demeanor.
3. How should you respond to others' criticism if you can no longer hold your tongue?

Conclusion:

Introduce the outline for the week as well as explain the daily exercises to be completed each day. Leaders, encourage everyone in the study group to complete their daily exercises and offer incentives to get more participation.

Outline for the Week

I.	Be Quick to Listen before Responding
II.	Let Silence be Your Friend
III.	Anger isn't Necessary
IV.	No Response is a Good Response
V.	Answer with Wisdom
VI.	Be a God-pleaser
VII.	Allow their Criticism to be Your Motivation

Group Session 3

Title: Gird Your Loins with Truth

Icebreaker Activity:

Allow one to two members to share one thing they had learned from the daily inspirational. (5 minutes)
Divide the group members into equal teams of three or four. Each team is to share the following information with the group: (10-15 minutes)

1. Are you afraid to tell people the truth?
2. How do you feel when others tell you the truth about yourself, especially behaviors you know you need to improve?
3. Are you a God-pleaser or a man-pleaser?

Scripture:

"God is not man that He should lie; neither the son of man that He should repent; has he said, and shall He not do it? Or Has He spoken, and shall He not make it good? Numbers 23:19 (KJV)

Introduction of the Lesson:

God does not lie and neither does His word come back void. His Word completes what it is sent out to do. Satan is the one who lies. He is actually the father of lies and no truth is in him. He uses lies to steal, kill, and destroy whatever we allow him.

It is your responsibility to know the truth. It is not the Pastor's responsibility to make sure you know the Word. Read God's Word for yourself. His Word is truth. *You must gird your loins with truth to stand firm against the wiles of the devil.* (Ephesians 6:14 KJV). You can't stand firm if you are not reading God's Word. The more you read God's Word, the stronger you will become against cynicism in today's society.

Discussion/Questions:

Don't be afraid to speak your truth. The truth which is collided with God's truth. The Word is written to be repeated and resounded in the atmosphere. *God says His word does not come back void and it will accomplish that which He purposed.* (Isaiah 55:11 ESV) So, speak His word to do what it is purposed to do. For an example, In First Samuel, the 17th chapter, and starting at verse 41, David is approaching the Philistine with a sling-shot in his hand. When the Philistine saw David, he disdained (disregard as if not worthy) him for David was young and ruddy. The Philistine said to David, *"Come to me so I can feed your flesh to the fowls of the air and the beasts of the field."* David replied, *"You come to me with a sword, spear, and javelin, but I come to you in the name of the Lord of hosts, the God of the armies of Israel, whom you have defied. On this day, the Lord will deliver you into my hands. I will smite you and cut your head off and give your body to the fowls of the air and the beasts of the field so that all the earth will know there is a God in Israel."*

Don't just read His Word, make it personal. Make it a habit. Make it a day to day job.

Ask the group the following questions and allow a few of the members to share their testimony:

What specific scripture have you utilize to fight the enemy which is Satan? What was the specific situation you wanted God to fight?

Conclusion:

Introduce the outline for the week as well as explain the daily exercises to be completed each day. Leaders, please encourage everyone in the study group to complete their daily exercises and offer incentives to get more participation.

Outline for the Week

I.   Be Lead in Truth
II. Speak Well of Yourself & Others
III. Be Accountable for Your Actions
IV. Choose Life not Death
V.   Be Yourself without Apology
VI. Silence Your Thoughts
VII. Think on These Things

Acknowledgments

I would like to take this moment to acknowledge a few family and friends who showed their utmost support for this God-given assignment. Jeffrey, my darling husband, you are phenomenal in so many ways. I thank you from the bottom of my heart for encouraging me when I wasn't my best. Margaret, my warrior mother, you made me feel like I could run a 5K Marathon. I thank you for showing your support and keeping me in your prayers. Karolyn, my Prayer Partner, you have such a big heart and God will reward you openly in front of all your friends and enemies. I thank you for showing your support and being there for me whenever I needed you. Neloise, you are an awesome Editor! I thank you so much for editing my book. I hope to return the favor. To all my children, plus NeNe, I thank you for being supportive as always. Last, but not least, to all the readers, thank you for being supportive and purchasing this book! I pray you were bless as much as I was writing this book!

www.ingramcontent.com/pod-product-compliance
Lightning Source LLC
Chambersburg PA
CBHW060122050426
42448CB00010B/1997